MASTER REINFORCEMEN[ ]THE ULTIMATE CRASH COURSE FOR BUSY PROFESSIONALS

WRITTEN BY EVAN WALTERS

Table of Contents

Preface

Welcome to the fast track of reinforcement learning (RL)! This book, "Master Reinforcement Learning: The Ultimate Crash Course for Busy Professionals," is designed to equip you, the time-crunched professional, with the essential knowledge and skills to leverage this powerful machine learning technique.

The world of artificial intelligence is rapidly evolving, and reinforcement learning stands at the forefront. It allows us to create intelligent agents that learn by interacting with their environment and receiving rewards. This approach mimics how humans learn through trial and error, making it incredibly versatile and applicable to a wide range of domains, from robotics and automation to finance and game development.

However, diving into reinforcement learning can be daunting. The technical jargon and complex algorithms might seem overwhelming at first. This crash course is here to bridge that gap. We'll cut through the noise and deliver the core concepts in a concise and easy-to-understand manner.

This book is specifically crafted for busy professionals like you. We understand your time is precious, so we've packed the content with actionable insights and practical examples. Each chapter focuses on a specific aspect of reinforcement learning, presented in a clear and structured format. We'll break down complex concepts into bite-sized pieces, utilizing real-world applications to illustrate their practical relevance.

By the end of this crash course, you'll be equipped with:

- A solid foundation in the core principles of reinforcement learning
- The ability to identify potential applications of RL in your field
- The confidence to implement basic reinforcement learning algorithms

No prior experience with machine learning is necessary. This book assumes only basic mathematical knowledge. With your dedication and this guide, you'll be well on your way to mastering reinforcement learning and unlocking its potential to transform your work.

So, are you ready to take the plunge? Let's dive into the exciting world of reinforcement learning!

Chapter 1: Demystifying Reinforcement Learning: From Theory to Applications

Imagine a scenario: you're tasked with training a robot to navigate a complex warehouse environment. You want it to efficiently pick up and deliver packages, avoiding obstacles and reaching its goals as quickly as possible. This is precisely where reinforcement learning (RL) comes in.

1.1 What is Reinforcement Learning and Why Should You Care?

Unlike traditional programming, where you explicitly instruct the robot on every step, RL takes a different approach. In the RL world, the robot (or "agent") learns through trial and error by interacting with its environment. It receives rewards for desired actions and penalties for mistakes, gradually refining its behavior to maximize the rewards it receives.

This ability to learn autonomously makes RL incredibly versatile. It can be applied to various tasks, including:

- **Robotics and Automation:** Training robots to perform complex tasks in dynamic environments, from manufacturing to search and rescue.
- **Game Development:** Creating intelligent AI opponents in games or designing agents that can master complex game environments.

- **Finance and Trading:** Developing algorithms that can make optimal investment decisions by analyzing market data and adapting to changing conditions.
- **Resource Management:** Optimizing resource allocation in complex systems, such as network traffic control or energy management.

These are just a few examples, and the potential applications of RL are constantly expanding.

1.2 Unveiling the Key Concepts: Agents, Environments, Rewards

At the heart of any RL system lies a three-way interaction:

- **Agent:** This is the decision-maker, the entity that interacts with the environment and learns from its experiences. In our warehouse example, the robot is the agent.

- **Environment:** This is the world the agent operates in. It provides the agent with information about its state (location of obstacles, packages, etc.) and responds to the agent's actions.
- **Reward:** This is the feedback mechanism that guides the agent's learning. Positive rewards encourage desired actions, while negative rewards penalize mistakes.

The RL agent continuously observes the environment, takes actions, receives rewards, and learns from these experiences. Over time, it optimizes its decision-making process to maximize the cumulative reward it receives.

1.3 Real-World Applications Across Industries: A Glimpse into the Future

The potential of reinforcement learning (RL) stretches far beyond the examples mentioned earlier. Let's explore some cutting-edge applications currently transforming various industries:

- **Healthcare:** Imagine RL algorithms assisting in drug discovery by simulating complex interactions between molecules. These agents could analyze vast datasets and identify potential drug candidates with minimal human intervention, accelerating the drug development process.

- **Manufacturing:** RL algorithms can optimize production lines in factories by dynamically adjusting machine settings and scheduling maintenance tasks. This can lead to increased efficiency, reduced downtime, and improved product quality.
- **Telecommunications:** RL is being used to manage network traffic congestion. These intelligent agents can analyze network data and dynamically adjust routing protocols to ensure smooth data flow and prevent network outages.
- **Cybersecurity:** RL algorithms can be trained to detect and respond to cyberattacks in real-time. By analyzing network traffic patterns, these agents can identify

suspicious activities and take preventative measures to safeguard critical infrastructure.

The future of RL holds even more exciting possibilities. Imagine personalized learning systems that adapt to individual student needs, or robots that can perform delicate surgeries with unmatched precision. With continued research and development, RL has the potential to revolutionize how we interact with machines and fundamentally change the world around us.

Beyond the Applications:

This glimpse into the future isn't just about specific applications. RL empowers us to automate tasks that were once considered too complex for computers. It allows us to create machines that can learn and adapt on their own, opening doors to entirely new avenues of innovation.

This chapter has hopefully sparked your curiosity about the potential of RL. As you delve deeper into this book, you'll gain the knowledge and skills to explore these possibilities yourself and contribute to the exciting future of reinforcement learning.

Chapter 2: Foundations of Reinforcement Learning: Building Your Toolkit

Welcome back! Now that you've grasped the core concepts of reinforcement learning (RL), it's time to build your foundational toolkit. This chapter equips you with the essential building blocks for understanding and implementing RL algorithms.

2.1 Introduction to Markov Decision Processes (MDPs): The Framework for Success

Remember the game "Rock, Paper, Scissors"? While seemingly simple, it actually embodies a core concept in reinforcement learning: Markov Decision Processes (MDPs). Imagine you're playing against an AI that learns from experience. MDPs provide the framework for structuring this scenario.

Understanding MDPs: A Structured Approach to Learning

An MDP essentially defines the world your RL agent operates in and the rules governing its interactions. It breaks down the decision-making process into four key elements:

1. **States (S):** These represent all the possible situations the agent can encounter. In "Rock, Paper, Scissors," there are three states: throwing rock, paper, or scissors.
2. **Actions (A):** These represent the choices the agent can make at each state. Here, the actions are throwing rock, paper, or scissors.

3. **Transition probabilities (P):** These define the likelihood of transitioning from one state (your throw) to another (opponent's throw) after taking a specific action (your choice). For instance, throwing rock might lead to a "rock vs. paper" state (opponent throws paper) with a 33% probability.
4. **Rewards (R):** These represent the feedback the agent receives for taking an action in a particular state. Winning a round might yield a positive reward (+1), while losing might incur a negative reward (-1).

Why MDPs Matter:

MDPs provide a structured way to model the interaction between the agent and its environment. This structure allows us to:

- **Formulate RL problems:** By defining the states, actions, transitions, and rewards, we can translate real-world problems into a language that RL algorithms can understand.
- **Develop optimal decision-making strategies:** MDPs allow us to define the goal (maximizing rewards) and design algorithms that help the agent learn the best course of action in each state.

Beyond "Rock, Paper, Scissors":

While the "Rock, Paper, Scissors" example is simplistic, MDPs can be applied to much more complex scenarios. Imagine training a robot to navigate a maze. Each location in the maze is a state, the robot's movement options are the actions, the transition probabilities define the likelihood of reaching a new location after a move, and the reward could be reaching the exit.

MDPs are a fundamental building block for understanding and implementing a wide range of reinforcement learning algorithms. By grasping this concept, you've taken a significant step towards mastering RL!

2.2 Understanding Rewards and Value Functions: Navigating the Learning Landscape

Imagine you're training a dog to fetch. You reward it with a treat for successfully retrieving the ball. This reward system is a simplified version of how reinforcement learning (RL) agents learn. But what guides them when rewards are delayed or uncertain? Here's where value functions come in.

Rewards: The Currency of Learning

In the world of RL, rewards are the driving force behind an agent's learning process. They act as feedback, indicating whether an action is leading the agent closer to its goal. Just like the treat motivates your dog, positive rewards in RL encourage the agent to repeat actions that lead to desirable outcomes. Conversely, negative rewards discourage actions that lead to undesirable outcomes.

However, rewards are often received in the future, not immediately after taking an action. This is especially true for complex tasks. For example, an RL agent training to play a game might not receive a reward (winning the game) until many moves later. So, how does the agent decide which actions to take in the present, knowing the reward is far off?

Enter Value Functions: A Compass for Future Rewards

A value function acts as a compass for the agent, estimating the long-term reward it can expect to receive by taking a specific action in a given state. Essentially, it helps the agent navigate the "learning landscape" by prioritizing actions that have the potential to lead to higher future rewards. Think of it like a map that shows the agent not just the immediate terrain but also the potential rewards (or pitfalls) that lie ahead.

There are different types of value functions, each with its own strengths and applications:

- **State-value function (V(s)):** This estimates the expected future reward the agent can receive starting from a particular state, regardless of the specific actions it takes.

- **Action-value function (Q(s,a)):** This estimates the expected future reward the agent can receive by taking a specific action (a) in a given state (s).

By estimating future rewards through value functions, the agent can make informed decisions in the present, even when the final outcome is uncertain.

The Power of Value Functions:

Value functions are crucial for RL algorithms because they:

- **Guide exploration:** They help the agent prioritize actions that have the potential to lead to higher rewards, encouraging exploration of the environment.
- **Enable optimal decision-making:** By comparing the value of different actions in a given state, the agent can choose the one with the highest expected future reward.
- **Facilitate learning from delayed rewards:** Value functions bridge the gap between immediate actions and

future rewards, allowing the agent to learn effectively even in complex scenarios.

In the next section, we'll delve deeper into the concept of policies and explore how they work with value functions to drive optimal decision-making in RL agents.

2.3 Policies and Exploration vs. Exploitation: Balancing Strategies for Optimal Performance

Imagine you're a taxi driver in a new city. You need to learn the best routes to navigate efficiently and maximize your fares (rewards). This scenario reflects the core challenge in reinforcement learning (RL): developing a strategy that balances exploration and exploitation.

Policies: The Agent's Decision-Making Compass

An RL agent's policy embodies its decision-making strategy. It defines the action the agent is most likely to take in a given state. Think of it as the taxi driver's mental map - a set of guidelines for choosing the most efficient route based on their current location.

The goal of RL is to find the optimal policy – the one that maximizes the agent's long-term reward. But achieving this optimal policy requires a delicate balance between two key strategies:

Exploration: This involves venturing into uncharted territory, trying out different actions to gather information about the environment and discover potentially high-reward states.

In the taxi analogy, exploration involves trying new shortcuts or routes during off-peak hours to see if they lead to faster travel times.

Exploitation: This involves focusing on actions that are known to lead to high rewards based on past experiences.

Sticking to well-known, efficient routes during peak hours would be an example of exploitation for the taxi driver.

Striking the Right Balance:

A successful RL agent needs to strike a balance between exploration and exploitation. Here's why:

- **Exploration is crucial for learning:** Without exploring new possibilities, the agent might miss out on high-reward states or more efficient ways to achieve its goals.
- **Exploitation maximizes immediate rewards:** Once the

agent has gained some knowledge of the environment, it should focus on exploiting this knowledge to maximize its immediate rewards.

The ideal balance between exploration and exploitation depends on several factors, including:

- **The complexity of the environment:** More complex environments might require more exploration initially.
- **The desired learning rate:** Striking a balance allows the agent to learn efficiently while still maximizing rewards.

Exploration Strategies:

There are various techniques to encourage exploration in RL:

- **Epsilon-greedy exploration:** This approach involves randomly choosing an action with a small probability (epsilon) to explore new options, even if they seem less optimal based on current knowledge.

- **Boltzmann exploration:** This method assigns a probability to each action based on its estimated value. Actions with higher values are more likely to be chosen, but there's still a chance of exploring less promising options.

The Takeaway:

By understanding policies and the importance of balancing exploration and exploitation, you've gained a deeper understanding of how RL agents learn to make optimal decisions in dynamic environments. In the coming chapters, we'll explore different RL algorithms that leverage these concepts to train agents to achieve their goals.

Chapter 3: Dynamic Programming for Reinforcement Learning: A Powerful Approach

Now that you've grasped the fundamental concepts of reinforcement learning (RL), it's time to delve into specific algorithms! This chapter explores Dynamic Programming (DP), a powerful approach for solving optimal control problems in environments with well-defined structures.

3.1 Unveiling Dynamic Programming: A Precise Path to Optimal Choices

Imagine you're a skilled chess player, strategically planning your next move to gain the upper hand. You consider all possible options, analyzing the potential consequences of each piece movement. This thought process aligns with Dynamic Programming (DP), a powerful technique for finding the optimal course of action in reinforcement learning (RL).

Breaking Down Complexities: The Core of DP

DP tackles problems by cleverly dividing them into smaller, more manageable subproblems. Like a skilled chef deconstructing a dish, DP breaks down the bigger picture into individual steps, allowing for a clearer path to the optimal solution.

In the context of RL, DP helps us find the ideal policy – the set of actions that leads the agent to the highest cumulative reward over time. Imagine an RL agent navigating a maze. DP can help it determine the best sequence of moves (policy) to reach the exit (goal) in the shortest time possible (maximizing reward).

Why Dynamic Programming? The Advantages

DP offers several advantages that make it a valuable tool in RL:

- **Guaranteed Optimality:** Under certain conditions, DP algorithms like Value Iteration can guarantee finding the absolute best solution – the policy that yields the highest long-term reward for the agent.
- **Structured Approach:** By breaking down complex problems into smaller, well-defined subproblems, DP provides a systematic approach to solving challenging RL tasks.
- **Theoretical Foundation:** DP is backed by a strong mathematical foundation,

making it a reliable and well-understood technique in the field of RL.

However, it's important to consider the limitations of DP as well:

- **Computational Cost:** As the number of states and actions in an RL problem grows, DP algorithms can become computationally expensive, requiring significant processing power and time to find the solution.
- **MDP Dependency:** DP relies heavily on the concept of Markov Decision Processes (MDPs), where the environment has well-defined states,

actions, transitions, and rewards (covered in Chapter 2). If an RL problem doesn't strictly adhere to an MDP structure, DP might not be the most suitable approach.

The Takeaway:

Dynamic Programming serves as a cornerstone for many RL algorithms. By understanding its core principles and both its strengths and limitations, you've gained a valuable perspective on how to find optimal solutions in structured RL environments. In the following chapters, we'll explore other algorithms that address different types of RL problems and go beyond the well-defined structure of MDPs.

3.2 Value Iteration: Iteratively Refining the Path to Reward

Remember the road trip analogy from the previous chapter? Imagine you're not just looking for the fastest route, but also considering scenic detours that might add some time but enhance the experience (reward). Value Iteration, a powerful Dynamic Programming (DP) algorithm, tackles this scenario effectively in the world of reinforcement learning (RL).

Unveiling Value Iteration: A Step-by-Step Approach

Value Iteration takes an iterative approach to finding the optimal policy for an RL agent. It progressively refines estimates of the value of each state, ultimately converging on the optimal values and the corresponding optimal policy. Here's a breakdown of the process:

1. **Initialization:** We begin by assigning an initial value (often zero) to every state in the environment. Think of it as a blank map where we'll gradually mark the value (reward

potential) of each location the agent encounters.

2. **Value Update:** The core of the algorithm lies in iteratively updating these state values. In each iteration, we consider each state and calculate the expected future reward the agent can achieve by taking every possible action from that state. We then update the state's value function with the highest expected reward it can potentially obtain.

Imagine the agent is at a junction in the road trip scenario. Value Iteration would consider taking the highway (fast but less scenic) or a scenic route (slower but more rewarding). It would then update the value of that junction state based on the option with the highest expected future reward (considering both travel time and scenic value).

3. **Policy Update:** Based on the updated value function, we can determine the best course of action (action with the highest expected future reward) for each state. This collection of preferred actions for each state forms the current policy. In our road trip example, the policy might favor the scenic route if the increase in scenic value

outweighs the additional travel time.

4. **Repeat:** The magic of Value Iteration lies in repetition. Steps 2 and 3 are repeated numerous times. With each iteration, the state value estimates and the policy become more refined, gradually converging towards the optimal solution.

Finding the Optimal Path:

Through this iterative process, Value Iteration eventually converges on the optimal value function, where each state accurately reflects its long-term reward potential. The corresponding policy, derived from the optimal value function, represents the sequence of actions that leads the agent to the highest cumulative reward over time.

The Strengths of Value Iteration:

- **Guaranteed Optimality:** Under certain conditions (specifically, for finite MDPs), Value Iteration is guaranteed to find the optimal policy, ensuring the agent achieves the maximum possible reward.
- **Systematic Updates:** The iterative approach provides a clear and systematic way to refine the value estimates and the policy, making it easier to understand and implement.

The Limitations to Consider:

- **Computational Cost:** As the number of states and actions in an RL problem grows, Value Iteration can become computationally expensive. The numerous iterations required for convergence can be resource-intensive.
- **MDP Dependence:** Like other DP algorithms, Value Iteration relies on a well-defined MDP structure, where the environment is fully observable and transitions are deterministic (refer to Chapter 2 for MDP details).

Value Iteration in Action:

Value Iteration is a fundamental algorithm in RL, particularly for problems with well-defined MDPs. While it might not be the most suitable choice for every scenario due to computational limitations, it provides a powerful tool for finding optimal policies and maximizing long-term rewards for RL agents.

In the next section, we'll explore another DP technique, Policy Iteration, which offers an alternative approach to finding optimal policies in RL.

3.3 Policy Iteration: A More Efficient Path to Improvement

Imagine you're a coach training a basketball team. You start with some basic plays, but as the season progresses, you refine your strategy based on the team's performance. Policy Iteration, a dynamic programming (DP) technique in reinforcement learning (RL), adopts a similar approach to finding an optimal policy.

Beyond Value Iteration: Exploring Policy Improvement

While Value Iteration iteratively refines value functions to find the optimal policy (Chapter 3.2), Policy Iteration takes a different approach.

It focuses directly on improving the policy itself, making it a computationally efficient alternative for specific scenarios.

Here's a breakdown of the Policy Iteration process:

1. **Start with Any Policy:** Unlike Value Iteration, which starts with blank state values, Policy Iteration begins with any initial policy, even a random one. This policy might not be optimal, but it serves as a starting point for improvement.

2. **Policy Evaluation:** The algorithm evaluates the current policy by calculating the expected value of each state

under that specific policy. Imagine evaluating each play in your basketball strategy by analyzing its success rate in leading to points.

3. **Policy Improvement:** Based on the evaluation, Policy Iteration identifies actions in each state that could lead to higher expected rewards. This is similar to analyzing your team's performance and identifying areas for improvement (e.g., switching to a different play in certain situations). The policy is then updated to favor these potentially better actions.

4. **Repeat:** Steps 2 and 3 are repeated until the policy converges (no further improvement is possible). Just like your basketball team keeps refining its strategies throughout the season, Policy Iteration continues to improve the policy until it reaches a stable state.

The Advantages of Policy Iteration:

- **Computational Efficiency:** Compared to Value Iteration, Policy Iteration can be computationally faster, especially for problems with large state spaces. It avoids the

numerous value function
updates required in Value
Iteration.

- **Simpler Implementation:** The
core concept of directly
improving the policy can be
easier to understand and
implement for certain
applications.

The Trade-Off: Optimality vs. Efficiency

However, there's a trade-off to
consider:

- **No Guaranteed Optimality:**
Unlike Value Iteration, Policy
Iteration doesn't guarantee
finding the absolute optimal

policy. It might converge to a locally optimal solution, which is good but not necessarily the absolute best.

Choosing the Right Tool:

The choice between Value Iteration and Policy Iteration depends on the specific RL problem:

- **For guaranteed optimality and well-defined MDPs:** Value Iteration might be preferred, especially for smaller problems.
- **For larger state spaces and situations where computational efficiency is a concern:** Policy Iteration can be a more practical choice,

even if it might not find the
absolute optimal solution.

The Takeaway:

Policy Iteration offers a valuable
alternative within the realm of
Dynamic Programming for RL.
While it might not guarantee the
absolute best solution, its
computational efficiency and focus
on directly improving the policy
make it a powerful tool for many
practical applications.

Looking Ahead:

In the coming chapters, we'll
venture beyond Dynamic
Programming and explore other RL
algorithms that address different

types of environments and learning scenarios. We'll delve into Monte Carlo methods, explore the power of deep learning in RL, and equip you with the knowledge to tackle a wider range of reinforcement learning challenges.

Chapter 4: Monte Carlo Methods: Learning from the Tapestry of Experience

Welcome back to the captivating realm of reinforcement learning (RL)! In the previous chapters, we delved into Dynamic Programming (DP) algorithms, which excel in well-defined environments with structured Markov Decision Processes (MDPs). However, many real-world scenarios are far more dynamic and unpredictable. This chapter ventures into the exciting realm of Monte Carlo (MC) methods, powerful tools that empower RL agents to learn and adapt through experience, even in complex and uncertain settings.

4.1 Embracing the Unknown: Overcoming the Limitations of MDPs

Imagine training a robot to navigate a bustling city street. Unlike the controlled mazes explored in earlier chapters, the environment here is brimming with uncertainty. Pedestrians dart across intersections, vehicles honk unexpectedly, and traffic lights change dynamically – these elements are difficult to capture within the rigid MDP framework. This is where Monte Carlo methods shine.

MC Methods: The Power of Learning by Doing

MC methods depart from the MDP dependency that characterizes DP algorithms. Instead of requiring complete knowledge of the environment's dynamics beforehand, they leverage the invaluable data collected through the agent's interactions with the world: the sequence of states, actions, and rewards it encounters. By meticulously analyzing this experience data (often gathered through simulations or real-world interactions), MC methods enable the agent to gradually learn and refine its decision-making capabilities.

Think of it like learning to ride a bicycle. You don't need a comprehensive understanding of physics or bicycle mechanics to become proficient. Through trial and error (experience), you learn to balance, steer, and eventually cruise confidently. MC methods embody this essence of experiential learning in the context of RL.

Code Example: Simulating a Simple Gridworld Environment (Python)

Python

```python
import numpy as np
```

```python
import random

class Gridworld:
    def __init__(self, size=4, goal=(0, 0), reward=-1,
wind_prob=0.1):
        self.size = size
        self.goal = goal
        self.reward = reward
        self.wind_prob = wind_prob
        self.state = (self.size // 2, self.size // 2)  #
Start in the center

    def move(self, action):
        # Define possible actions (up, down, left, right)
        actions = [(0, 1), (0, -1), (1, 0), (-1, 0)]
        new_state = tuple(map(sum, zip(self.state,
actions[action])))

        # Handle boundaries and wind effects
        new_state = (max(0, min(new_state[0], self.size -
1)),
                     max(0, min(new_state[1], self.size -
1)))
        if random.random() < self.wind_prob:  # Simulate
wind pushing up
            new_state = (new_state[0], min(new_state[1] + 1,
self.size - 1))

        # Check for goal and return reward
        if new_state == self.goal:
            return self.goal, self.reward
        else:
            return new_state, -1  # Penalty for non-goal
states

    def reset(self):
        self.state = (self.size // 2, self.size // 2)
        return self.state

# Example usage
env = Gridworld()
```

```
state = env.reset()
done = False
while not done:
  # Choose an action (e.g., using an RL policy)
  action = ...
  next_state, reward, done = env.move(action)
  # Update the agent's knowledge based on experience
(reward)
  # ...
```

4.2 Unveiling the Power of MC Prediction: Estimating State Values

One core application of MC methods in RL is state value prediction. The goal is to estimate the expected future reward (value) an agent can anticipate from a particular state, given the current policy it follows. Here, we delve into two primary approaches within MC prediction:

- **Episode MC:** This method considers the entire return (sum of rewards) received by the agent in an episode (a complete interaction sequence from start to finish). Imagine the total reward received throughout a single bike ride (from starting off wobbly to riding smoothly) – that's the episode return in this scenario.

Python

```python
def episode_mc_prediction(
```

4.3 Q-Learning: A Powerful Monte Carlo Technique for Optimal Control

In our exploration of Monte Carlo (MC) methods, we've seen how they empower agents to learn from experience, even in complex environments. Now, we delve into a particularly powerful MC technique: Q-Learning.

Unveiling Q-Learning: The Core of Off-Policy Learning

Q-Learning stands out as a key player in the realm of RL due to its ability to learn an optimal policy (strategy) for maximizing rewards, even when the data it learns from wasn't generated by the current policy being evaluated. This is known as **off-policy learning**, and it sets Q-Learning apart from some other MC methods.

Imagine you're training a robot dog to fetch. You can demonstrate good fetching behavior (the optimal policy) or let it explore on its own (a different policy). Q-Learning allows the robot dog to learn from both scenarios, eventually converging on the optimal fetching strategy (maximizing the reward of praise or treats).

The Core of Q-Learning: Updating Q-Values

Q-Learning revolves around the concept of Q-values, which represent the estimated **expected future reward** an agent can anticipate by taking a specific action (a) in a particular state (s).

The core idea lies in iteratively updating these Q-values based on the agent's experiences. Here's the update rule:

```
Q(s, a) <- Q(s, a) + α [R + γ * max(Q(s', a')) - Q(s, a)]
```

- **Q(s, a):** The Q-value for taking action a in state s (being updated)
- **α (alpha):** The learning rate (0 < α <= 1), controls how much the agent prioritizes new experiences vs. past knowledge
- **R:** The immediate reward received after taking action a in state s

- **γ (gamma):** The discount factor $(0 <= \gamma < 1)$, determines the importance of future rewards. Lower values emphasize immediate rewards, while higher values prioritize long-term gains.
- **s':** The state the agent transitions to after taking action a in state s
- **a':** The action the agent might take in state s' (considering the best possible future reward)
- **max(Q(s', a')):** Represents the estimated future reward obtainable by taking the best possible action in the new state s'

Breaking Down the Update Rule:

1. **Experience Accumulation:** The agent interacts with the environment, taking actions and receiving rewards.

2. **Q-Value Update:** For the current state (s) and action (a), the Q-value is updated based on four key factors:

    - **Previous Q-value (Q(s, a)):** This represents the agent's prior knowledge about the value of taking action a in state s.

    - **Learning Rate (α):** This factor controls how much the agent prioritizes the newly acquired experience

$(R + γ * max(Q(s', a')))$
compared to its past
knowledge $(Q(s, a))$.

- **Immediate Reward (R):**
  This reflects the immediate
  reward the agent received
  after taking action a in state
  s.
- **Future Reward Estimation
  $(γ * max(Q(s', a')))$:** This
  term considers the
  estimated future reward the
  agent can expect by taking
  the best possible action (a')
  in the new state (s') it
  transitioned to. The discount
  factor (γ) determines how
  much weight is given to this

future reward compared to the immediate reward.

The Power of Q-Learning:

Q-Learning offers several advantages:

- **Off-Policy Learning:** It can learn from experience data generated by different policies, not just the current one. This is valuable for scenarios where directly implementing the optimal policy might be difficult or impractical.
- **Sample-Based Learning:** Q-Learning learns from individual experiences (samples) rather than requiring

complete knowledge of the environment. This makes it suitable for complex and dynamic settings.

- **Simple and Flexible Implementation:** The core Q-learning update rule is relatively straightforward to implement and can be adapted to various RL problems.

Considerations to Keep in Mind:

- **Exploration vs. Exploitation:** Q-Learning requires a balance between exploration (trying new actions) and exploitation (focusing on actions with high Q-values). Techniques like epsilon-greedy exploration (randomly choosing actions with a small probability) can be employed.

- **Convergence:** While Q-Learning typically converges to an optimal policy under certain conditions, the learning process can be slow, especially in large environments.

Code Example: Implementing Q-Learning in Python (Gridworld Example)

Python

```python
import numpy as np

class QLearningAgent:
    def __init__(self,
```

Chapter 5:
Temporal-Difference Learning: Bridging the Gap

As we delve deeper into the realm of reinforcement learning (RL), we encounter the fascinating concept of Temporal-Difference (TD) learning. TD methods bridge the gap between Monte Carlo (MC) methods (focusing on episode returns) and value function estimation techniques. Let's embark on a journey to understand the essence of TD learning and explore its applications in RL.

5.1 Unveiling the Power of TD Learning: Beyond Episode Returns

Imagine you're training a self-driving car. In MC methods, the car would need to complete an entire trip (episode) before learning the value of each state (e.g., a busy intersection). This can be inefficient, especially for long journeys. TD learning offers a more time-sensitive approach.

The Core Idea: Learning from Single Steps

TD learning methods don't wait for the entire episode to be completed before updating their estimates. Instead, they leverage the current state, the action taken, the immediate reward received, and an estimate of the future reward to update the value of the current state. This enables faster learning and adaptation compared to MC methods that rely solely on episode returns.

Think of the self-driving car again. With TD learning, the car can learn the value of being at a busy intersection (a state) based on the immediate reward (e.g., time spent waiting) and an estimate of the future reward (reaching the destination smoothly). It doesn't need to wait for the entire trip to be finished.

5.2 TD(0): A Fundamental Approach

One of the simplest TD methods is TD(0). The update rule for TD(0) is as follows:

```
V(s) <- V(s) + α [R + γ * V(s') - V(s)]
```

- **V(s):** The value of the current state (s) being updated
- **α (alpha):** The learning rate (0 < α <= 1), controls how much the agent prioritizes the new experience vs. past knowledge
- **R:** The immediate reward received after taking an action in state s
- **γ (gamma):** The discount factor (0 <= γ < 1), determines the importance of future rewards.

Lower values emphasize immediate rewards, while higher values prioritize long-term gains.

- **V(s'):** The estimated value of the next state (s') reached after taking an action in state s

Understanding the Update Rule:

1. **Experience Accumulation:** The agent interacts with the environment, taking actions and receiving rewards.
2. **Value Update:** For the current state (s), the value (V(s)) is updated based on three key factors:
   - **Previous Value (V(s)):** This represents the agent's prior

knowledge about the value of state s.

- **Learning Rate (α):** This factor controls how much the agent prioritizes the newly acquired experience $(R + γ * V(s'))$ compared to its past knowledge $(V(s))$.
- **Immediate Reward and Future Reward Estimate $(R + γ * V(s'))$:** This term incorporates both the immediate reward (R) received and an estimate of the future reward $(γ * V(s'))$ obtainable by reaching the next state (s').

The Advantages of TD(0):

- **Faster Learning:** By not waiting for episode completion, TD(0) can learn more rapidly than MC methods, especially in large or complex environments.
- **Bootstrapping:** TD(0) leverages bootstrapping, a technique where current estimates are used to improve future estimates. This can accelerate learning by utilizing the agent's current understanding of the environment.

The Considerations to Keep in Mind:

- **Convergence:** TD(0) might not always converge to the optimal value function under certain conditions. However, it can still learn effective policies in many practical scenarios.

- **On-Policy Learning:** The basic TD(0) method typically requires data generated by the current policy being evaluated.

5.3 SARSA (State-Action-Reward-State-Action): Combining Control and Prediction

SARSA is a popular TD control method that builds upon TD(0). It introduces the concept of following a specific policy (e.g., an epsilon-greedy policy) while learning. Here's the update rule for SARSA:

```
Q(s, a) <- Q(s, a) + α [R + γ * Q(s', a') - Q(s, a)]
```

- **Q(s, a):** The Q-value for taking action a in state s (being updated)
- **α (alpha):** The learning rate (0 < α <= 1)
- **R:** The immediate reward received after taking

Chapter 6 Deep Reinforcement Learning: The Power of Neural Networks

In this chapter, we delve into the exciting intersection of deep learning and reinforcement learning, a powerful combination that unlocks remarkable capabilities for RL agents. Here's what you can expect to learn:

1. Limitations of Traditional RL Methods:

- Traditional RL algorithms like Q-learning and SARSA can struggle with high-dimensional state spaces or complex tasks where representing the value function for every possible state-action pair becomes impractical.

- The curse of dimensionality can hinder the performance of traditional methods in large and complex environments.

2. Deep Q-Networks (DQNs): A Game Changer

- DQN introduces the revolutionary concept of using deep neural networks to represent the value function (Q-value) for an action in a given state. This allows the agent to learn complex relationships between states and actions, even in high-dimensional environments.

- The chapter will likely explain the architecture of a DQN, including convolutional neural networks (CNNs) for processing visual inputs and recurrent neural networks (RNNs) for handling sequential data.

- You'll learn about experience replay, a crucial technique for training DQN agents effectively by leveraging past experiences stored in a replay buffer.

3. Policy Gradient Methods with Deep Neural Networks:

- The chapter might explore how deep neural networks can be

employed to represent the policy function ($\pi(a|s)$) directly. This enables learning complex policies for continuous control tasks or situations with large action spaces.

- Actor-Critic methods with deep neural networks, such as Deep Deterministic Policy Gradients (DDPG), will likely be discussed. DDPG utilizes separate deep neural networks for the actor (policy) and critic (value function), achieving efficient learning in continuous control domains.

4. Advantages of Deep Reinforcement Learning:

- The ability to handle high-dimensional state spaces and complex tasks.
- Generalization: Deep RL agents can learn policies that apply to unseen states based on the patterns learned from the training data.
- Potential for sample efficiency: Deep neural networks can extract meaningful patterns from data, potentially requiring less training data compared to traditional RL methods.

5. Challenges and Considerations:

- Training deep RL models can be computationally expensive,

requiring powerful hardware resources (GPUs).

- Exploration vs. exploitation dilemma remains crucial in deep RL, as agents need to balance exploring new actions with exploiting the actions known to be beneficial.
- The interpretability and explainability of deep RL models can be challenging, limiting our understanding of how the agent arrives at its decisions.

6. Conclusion:

Deep reinforcement learning represents a transformative force in the field of RL. By leveraging the power of neural networks, RL agents can tackle problems previously deemed intractable. The chapter will likely conclude by discussing the ongoing research in deep RL and its promising future applications in various domains like robotics, game playing, and autonomous systems.

6.1 Unleashing the Power of Deep Learning: Reinforcement Meets Artificial Neural Networks

Welcome to the fascinating realm of Deep Reinforcement Learning (DRL)! In this chapter, we'll witness the magic that unfolds when the principles of reinforcement learning (RL) and the prowess of artificial neural networks (ANNs) converge. Get ready to explore how DRL empowers agents to conquer complex environments that leave traditional RL methods bewildered.

The Intrigue of Complex Environments

Imagine training a self-driving car to navigate a bustling city. Traditional RL methods might struggle in this scenario due to the environment's complexity. Here's why:

- **High-Dimensional State Spaces:** The car encounters a vast amount of information through its cameras and sensors. This creates a high-dimensional state space, making it challenging for traditional RL to represent and reason about effectively.
- **Continuous Action Spaces:** Steering a car involves nuanced control, not just a set of discrete actions (left, right). This continuous nature of the action space can be difficult for traditional RL to handle.
- **Partially Observable Environments:** The car might not have a complete view of its

surroundings (e.g., hidden by buildings). This partial observability creates an additional hurdle for traditional RL to make optimal decisions.

The Power of Deep Learning Comes to the Rescue

This is where Deep Reinforcement Learning (DRL) steps in, wielding the power of artificial neural networks (ANNs) to address these challenges. Here's how DRL makes a difference:

- **Function Approximation with ANNs:** DRL leverages ANNs, with their ability to learn complex patterns from data, to approximate essential RL functions like value functions and policies. These functions map states to rewards or actions, guiding the agent's decision-making.

- **Learning from Raw Sensory Inputs:** Unlike traditional RL methods that might rely on hand-crafted features, DRL allows agents to learn directly from raw sensory data (images, sensor readings) through ANNs. This eliminates the need for intricate feature engineering and enables the agent to discover relevant patterns on its own.

- **Handling High-Dimensional Data:** ANNs excel at processing high-dimensional data. They can effectively extract meaningful features from complex state spaces, empowering the agent to navigate environments with rich sensory information.

In essence, DRL bridges the gap between the raw sensory data of the real world and the decision-making requirements of RL. By allowing agents to learn intricate patterns directly from experience, DRL unlocks the potential for remarkable

achievements in various domains.

The Broader Landscape of DRL Architectures

While Deep Q-Networks (DQNs) will be explored in detail in the next section, it's important to acknowledge the broader landscape of DRL architectures. Here are some prominent examples:

- **Deep Deterministic Policy Gradients (DDPG):** Well-suited for continuous control tasks where the agent has a vast range of possible actions.

- **Policy Gradient Methods with Actor-Critic (A3C):** Efficiently handle parallel training across multiple agents or environments.
- **Proximal Policy Optimization (PPO):** Addresses potential instability issues that can arise in some policy gradient methods.

As we delve deeper into DRL, we'll encounter these architectures and explore their unique strengths and applications.

Get ready to witness the power of deep learning revolutionizing the field of reinforcement learning!

6.2 Deep Q-Networks (DQNs): Mastering Complex Environments through Deep Learning

Deep Q-Networks (DQNs) stand as a pioneering architecture in Deep Reinforcement Learning (DRL), paving the way for many advancements in the field. In this section, we'll delve into the core concepts of DQNs and how they empower agents to excel in complex environments that leave traditional RL methods behind.

The Synergy of Q-Learning and Deep Neural Networks

DQNs essentially combine the well-established Q-learning algorithm (introduced in Chapter

4.3) with the power of deep neural networks. As a reminder, Q-learning focuses on learning the Q-value, which represents the expected future reward an agent can anticipate by taking a specific action (a) in a particular state (s).

The magic of DQNs lies in replacing the traditional Q-value table with a deep neural network (DQN). This network has the remarkable ability to learn complex, non-linear relationships between states, actions, and future rewards, even in high-dimensional environments.

The DQN Architecture: Learning from Experience

The DQN architecture typically consists of the following components:

1. **Input Layer:** This layer receives the state (s) of the environment as input. The state representation can be raw sensory data (e.g., image from a camera) or processed features depending on the specific scenario.

2. **Hidden Layers:** These layers are the heart of the DQN, where the neural network's magic happens. They contain a large number of interconnected artificial neurons that process the input from the previous

layer and extract increasingly complex features from the state representation. The number of hidden layers and neurons within them can vary depending on the complexity of the environment.

3. **Output Layer:** This layer produces the Q-values for all possible actions (a) that the agent can take in the current state (s). The DQN learns to map the input state to these Q-values, essentially predicting the expected future reward for each action.

The Learning Process: Updating the Q-Values

DQNs leverage the Q-learning update rule (introduced in Chapter 4.3) to iteratively improve their estimates of the Q-values. Here's a breakdown of the update process:

1. **Experience Replay:** DQNs often utilize experience replay, a technique where the agent stores its experiences (state transitions, actions, rewards) in a memory buffer. This buffer is then randomly sampled during the learning process, allowing the DQN to learn from a diverse set of experiences and avoid overfitting to specific sequences.

2. **Mini-Batch Updates:** The DQN samples a mini-batch of experiences from the replay memory. For each experience (s, a, R, s'), the Q-value for the chosen action (a) in the current state (s) is updated using the Q-learning update rule. The target value for the update incorporates the Q-value of the next state (s') and the immediate reward (R) received.

The Power of DQNs: Conquering Complex Environments

DQNs offer several advantages that make them well-suited for complex environments:

- **Function Approximation:** The DQN can approximate complex value functions, even in high-dimensional state spaces. This eliminates the need for hand-crafted features and allows the agent to learn directly from raw sensory inputs.
- **Continuous Learning:** Through experience replay, DQNs can learn from a vast amount of data, continuously refining their Q-value estimates and improving their decision-making over time.
- **Adaptability:** DQNs can be applied to a wide range of environments, from Atari games

(where the state is an image) to robot control tasks (where the state is sensor readings).

DQNs: A Stepping Stone to Further Exploration

While DQNs have revolutionized DRL, they are not without limitations. They can be computationally expensive to train, and their performance can be sensitive to hyperparameter tuning. However, DQNs provide a foundational framework upon which many advanced DRL architectures are built. As we delve deeper into DRL, we'll explore these advancements and how they address some of the shortcomings of DQNs.

In conclusion, Deep Q-Networks (DQNs) represent a landmark achievement in DRL, demonstrating the power of deep learning to empower agents to conquer complex environments that were previously intractable for traditional RL methods.

6.3 Beyond Deep Q-Networks: Exploring Advanced Architectures for Deep Reinforcement Learning

1. Limitations of DQNs:

- The chapter might begin by revisiting some limitations of DQNs:
  - **Overestimation Bias:** DQNs can be prone to overestimating Q-values, leading to suboptimal policies. Techniques like Double DQN and Dueling DQN are introduced to mitigate this issue.
- **Sample Inefficiency:** Training DQN agents can still require a significant amount of data, especially in complex environments.

2. Advanced DQN Architectures:

- The chapter will likely explore advancements built upon the DQN architecture:
  - **Dueling DQN:** This architecture separates the value function ($V(s)$) from the advantage function ($A(s, a)$), potentially improving learning efficiency.
  - **Prioritized Experience Replay:** Prioritizing important experiences in the replay buffer based on a metric like novelty or TD-error can improve learning speed.

3. Actor-Critic Methods with Deep Networks:

- As an alternative to value-based methods like DQN, the chapter might introduce Actor-Critic methods using deep neural networks:
  - **Deep Deterministic Policy Gradients (DDPG):** This approach utilizes separate actor and critic networks, both employing deep neural networks. The actor learns a deterministic policy for continuous control tasks, while the critic evaluates the state-action value.
  - **Twin Delayed Deep Deterministic Policy Gradients (TD3):** This builds upon DDPG by

introducing techniques like target networks and delayed policy updates to improve stability and learning efficiency.

4. Attention Mechanisms in Deep RL:

- Similar to their application in supervised learning, attention mechanisms can be incorporated into DRL architectures to focus on crucial parts of the state space when making decisions. This can be particularly beneficial in environments with high-dimensional visual inputs.

5. Hierarchical Reinforcement Learning:

- For complex tasks that can be decomposed into subtasks, hierarchical RL approaches using deep networks can be introduced. This allows the agent to learn high-level goals and delegate subtasks to lower-level policies.

6. Exploration vs. Exploitation in Deep RL:

- This section might revisit the ongoing challenge of balancing exploration (trying new actions) and exploitation (utilizing known good actions). Techniques like epsilon-greedy exploration or UCB (Upper Confidence Bound) strategies can be explored.

7. Conclusion:

The chapter likely concludes by emphasizing the ongoing research and development in advanced DRL architectures. New architectures and techniques are constantly emerging, pushing the boundaries of what RL agents can achieve.

Additional Considerations:

- The chapter might touch upon challenges like computational complexity and the need for significant training data when using deep neural networks in RL.

- Brief discussions on potential applications of these advanced DRL architectures in various domains like robotics, game playing, and resource management could be included.

By exploring these advanced architectures, you'll gain a deeper understanding of the capabilities and potential of Deep Reinforcement Learning.

Chapter 7: Putting Reinforcement Learning into Practice: Implementation Essentials

Welcome to the practical realm of reinforcement learning (RL)! In this chapter, we'll equip you with the essential knowledge to implement RL algorithms and witness their capabilities firsthand. We'll delve into core concepts like environment setup, agent design, training considerations, and evaluation techniques, empowering you to embark on your own RL adventures.

7.1 Choosing the Right Tools: Libraries and Frameworks for Building RL Agents

Equipping yourself with the proper toolkit is essential for venturing into the realm of reinforcement learning (RL) agent development. This section delves into the valuable libraries and frameworks that empower you to construct, train, and evaluate your RL agents.

Popular Open-Source Libraries and Frameworks

Here's a selection of widely used open-source libraries and

frameworks that can significantly enhance your RL development experience:

1. OpenAI Gym:

- A cornerstone toolkit for developing and comparing RL algorithms.
- Offers a comprehensive suite of environments encompassing classic control tasks, Atari games, robotics simulations, and more.
- Provides a standardized interface for interacting with environments, making it easy to implement and test your RL algorithms.

2. TensorFlow/PyTorch:

- Deep learning frameworks forming the foundation for building powerful RL agents with neural networks.
- TensorFlow (TF) and PyTorch (PyTorch) offer extensive capabilities for constructing, training, and deploying deep neural networks.
- Both frameworks provide libraries specifically designed for reinforcement learning tasks, such as TensorFlow Agents (TF-Agents) and PyTorch's integration with

popular RL libraries like Stable Baselines3.

3. Stable Baselines3:

- A high-level open-source library built on top of PyTorch, specifically designed for streamlining RL development.
- Offers implementations of various well-established RL algorithms, including DQN, PPO, A2C, and SAC, readily available for use.
- Provides tools for simplifying the training process, such as hyperparameter tuning, experience replay, and policy evaluation.

4. RLlib (by Ray):

- A versatile library offering both high-level and low-level RL APIs.
- Supports various policy algorithms, execution modes (local, distributed), and integrations with popular frameworks like TensorFlow and PyTorch.
- Well-suited for complex RL projects requiring customization and fine-grained control over the learning process.

5. Dopamine (by Google Research):

- A research framework geared towards rapid prototyping and experimentation with RL algorithms.
- Offers a modular design, allowing researchers to easily swap components and experiment with different RL approaches.
- Less focused on large-scale deployments compared to other libraries, but valuable for research and exploration of new RL concepts.

Choosing the Right Tool for You:

The optimal library or framework for your project depends on several factors:

- **Project Complexity:** For simpler environments and algorithms, OpenAI Gym and Stable Baselines3 might suffice. For large-scale or research-oriented projects, RLlib or Dopamine could be better suited.
- **Deep Learning Experience:** If you're comfortable with deep learning frameworks like TensorFlow or PyTorch, leveraging their RL libraries

offers a high degree of flexibility and customization.

- **Ease of Use:** Stable Baselines3 prioritizes ease of use with pre-built implementations, while RLlib offers more control but with a steeper learning curve.

Additional Considerations:

- **Community and Documentation:** Look for libraries with active communities and comprehensive documentation for support and learning opportunities.

- **Scalability and Performance:** Consider the scalability of the library to handle complex environments and potentially large-scale training tasks.

By carefully evaluating your project's requirements and your own skillset, you can select the most appropriate tool from this rich ecosystem of open-source RL libraries and frameworks. With the right tools in hand, you'll be well-equipped to embark on your journey of building and training effective RL agents!

7.2 Building Your First Reinforcement Learning Agent: A Hands-on Example

Welcome to the exciting world of hands-on reinforcement learning (RL)! In this section, we'll guide you through building your very first RL agent using a popular open-source library – Stable Baselines3 (SB3). We'll focus on a classic environment – the CartPole problem – where the agent learns to balance a pole on a moving cart.

Before We Begin:

- Ensure you have Python installed along with the

necessary libraries: `pip install gym[all] stable-baselines3`

- This example assumes basic familiarity with Python programming concepts.

1. Importing Libraries and Defining the Environment:

Python

```python
import gym
from stable_baselines3 import PPO

env = gym.make('CartPole-v1')
```

Here, we import the necessary libraries: `gym` for interacting with the environment and `PPO` from Stable Baselines3 for our RL algorithm (Proximal Policy

Optimization). We then create an instance of the CartPole environment using `gym.make`.

2. Creating the RL Agent:

Python

```
model = PPO('MlpPolicy', env, verbose=1)
```

This line creates our RL agent using the `PPO` class from SB3. We specify the policy architecture (`MlpPolicy` – a Multilayer Perceptron) and the environment (`env`). The `verbose=1` parameter provides basic logging information during training.

3. Training the Agent:

```python
model.learn(total_timesteps=25000)
```

This line initiates the training process. We set the `total_timesteps` parameter to 25000, which defines the total number of steps (interactions between the agent and the environment) for which the agent will train. SB3 will handle the training loop internally, optimizing the agent's policy based on the rewards it receives in the environment.

4. Evaluating the Agent:

```python
obs = env.reset()
```

```
for _ in range(1000):
    action, _ = model.predict(obs)
    obs, reward, done, info = env.step(action)
    env.render()
    if done:
        break
env.close()
```

Here, we evaluate the agent's performance. We first reset the environment (`env.reset()`) to get the initial observation (`obs`). The loop runs for 1000 steps. Inside the loop:

- `model.predict(obs)` queries the agent for the best action based on the current observation (`obs`).
- The agent takes the predicted action (`action`) in the environment using

`env.step(action)`. This step returns the new observation (`obs`), reward (`reward`), done flag (`done` indicating episode completion), and additional info (`info`).

- The environment is rendered visually (`env.render()`) to observe the agent's performance.
- The loop breaks (`break`) if the episode terminates (`done`).

Running the Code:

Save the code snippets above in a Python script (e.g., `cartpole_ppo.py`) and execute it from your terminal using `python cartpole_ppo.py`. You'll see training progress messages during the training phase. Once training is complete, the script will render the environment and showcase the agent's balancing skills!

Beyond the Basics:

This example provides a foundational understanding of building an RL agent with Stable Baselines3. SB3 offers various functionalities for customization, such as hyperparameter tuning and saving/loading trained models. Explore the Stable

Baselines3 documentation for further details and delve into more complex environments and algorithms as you progress on your RL journey!

7.3 Debugging and Optimizing Your RL Systems: Ensuring Efficient Learning

Training an RL agent can be an iterative process. Just like any complex system, RL agents can encounter issues that hinder their learning progress. This section equips you with valuable techniques for debugging and optimizing your RL systems, ensuring efficient learning and achieving optimal performance.

Common Challenges in RL Training:

Here are some frequent hurdles you might encounter while training your RL agent:

- **Poor Performance:** The agent might not exhibit significant improvement in reward or fail to achieve the desired goal.
- **Unstable Training:** The agent's performance might fluctuate significantly during

training, hindering convergence.

- **Sample Inefficiency:** The agent might not learn effectively from the experiences it collects, leading to slow progress.

Debugging Strategies:

- **Visualize the Training Process:** Monitor key metrics like episode reward, loss function, and exploration rate over time. This visualization can help identify trends and potential issues.
- **Evaluate Agent Behavior:** Observe how the agent

interacts with the environment. Look for signs of getting stuck in local optima or making nonsensical decisions.

- **Analyze Experience Replay Buffer:** If using experience replay, ensure the buffer contains diverse experiences and is not dominated by irrelevant or outdated data.

Optimization Techniques:

- **Hyperparameter Tuning:** Experiment with different settings for hyperparameters like learning rate, discount factor, and exploration rate.

Techniques like grid search or random search can aid in finding optimal configurations.

- **Reward Shaping:** Carefully design the reward function to guide the agent towards the desired behavior. Consider providing intermediate rewards for achieving subgoals or penalizing undesirable actions.

- **Exploration vs. Exploitation Balance:** Employ strategies like ε-greedy exploration to ensure the agent explores new actions while also focusing on actions with high expected rewards.

Additional Tips:

- **Start Simple:** Begin with simpler environments and algorithms before tackling complex problems. This allows you to isolate and address potential issues more easily.

- **Leverage Pre-trained Models:** Consider using pre-trained models as a starting point, especially for complex environments. Fine-tuning a pre-trained model can often be more efficient than training from scratch.

- **Utilize Debugging Tools:** Many RL libraries offer debugging tools that can help you visualize the agent's internal state, value estimates, and policy decisions.

Remember: Debugging and optimizing RL systems is an ongoing process. Experimentation, analysis, and refinement are crucial for achieving successful learning outcomes. By employing the techniques mentioned above, you can ensure your RL systems learn efficiently and reach their full potential.

Moving Forward:

As you explore the exciting world of RL, keep in mind that successful development involves not just building the agent but also carefully crafting the environment, reward function, and training process. Embrace the iterative nature of RL, and leverage debugging and optimization techniques to create high-performing RL agents that can tackle challenging tasks!

Chapter 8: Advanced Topics in Reinforcement Learning: Expanding Your Horizons

Having grasped the core concepts and explored powerful techniques like Deep Q-Networks (DQNs) and advanced DRL architectures, Chapter 8 ventures into exciting frontiers of reinforcement learning (RL). This chapter serves as a springboard for delving deeper into specialized areas and equipping you to tackle even more intricate RL challenges. Here's a glimpse of what you might encounter:

8.1 Policy Gradients: Learning Directly from Policy Space

Policy gradients represent a powerful approach in reinforcement learning (RL) that allows the agent to learn directly by modifying its policy in the policy space. Unlike methods like Q-learning that focus on learning value functions, policy gradients directly optimize the policy function itself, leading the agent towards actions that generate higher rewards in the long run.

Core Concepts:

- **Policy Space:** This space encompasses all possible

policies the agent can adopt, represented mathematically by $\pi(a|s)$. Here, π represents the policy, a denotes an action, and s represents a state. The policy $\pi(a|s)$ defines the probability of taking action a in state s.

- **Policy Gradient:** This refers to the change in the policy based on the reward signal received by the agent. The goal is to update the policy in a direction that increases the expected future reward.
- **Gradient Estimation:** A crucial aspect of policy

gradients involves estimating the gradient of the expected future reward with respect to the policy parameters. This gradient indicates how changing the policy will impact the agent's long-term reward.

Benefits of Policy Gradients:

- **Direct Policy Optimization:** Policy gradients directly modify the agent's behavior, potentially leading to faster learning in certain scenarios.
- **Continuous Action Spaces:** Well-suited for environments with continuous action spaces

(e.g., robot control tasks) where representing a value function for every possible action might be impractical.

Challenges of Policy Gradients:

- **Variance:** Estimating the policy gradient can be challenging due to the inherent variance in the reward signal. Techniques like baseline subtraction can help mitigate this issue.
- **Sample Inefficiency:** Policy gradients might require a large number of samples (interactions with the

environment) to learn effectively, especially in complex environments.

Popular Policy Gradient Algorithms:

- **REINFORCE:** A foundational policy gradient algorithm that utilizes the episodic return (sum of rewards in an episode) for gradient estimation.

- **Proximal Policy Optimization (PPO):** Addresses potential instability issues that can arise in some policy gradient methods by

introducing a clipped
objective function.

- **Actor-Critic (A3C):** Employs
an actor-critic architecture
where the actor learns the
policy and the critic evaluates
the value of the actions taken
by the actor. This combined
approach can improve
learning efficiency.

Summary:

Policy gradients offer a
compelling approach to
reinforcement learning by directly
optimizing the agent's policy in
the policy space. While
challenges like variance and

sample inefficiency exist, policy gradients have led to the development of powerful RL algorithms that are well-suited for various tasks, particularly those involving continuous control in complex environments.

In the next section, we'll delve deeper into Deep Q-Networks (DQNs), which combine the power of deep learning with value function learning for remarkable achievements in RL.

8.2 Actor-Critic Methods: Combining Policy Gradients and Value Functions

Actor-critic methods stand out in reinforcement learning (RL) by merging the strengths of policy gradients and value function learning. This powerful combination addresses some limitations inherent in each individual approach and unlocks new avenues for effective RL agent development.

Core Idea:

The core idea behind actor-critic methods lies in employing two separate components within the agent:

- **Actor:** This component focuses on learning and improving the policy function ($\pi(a|s)$), similar to policy gradient methods. The actor directly interacts with the environment, taking actions and receiving rewards.
- **Critic:** This component acts as an evaluator, estimating the value function ($Q(s, a)$) that represents the expected future reward for taking action a in state s. The critic leverages the rewards

received by the agent to refine its value estimates.

The Learning Process:

The actor and critic work together in an iterative fashion:

1. **Actor Takes Action:** The actor selects an action based on the current policy.
2. **Critic Evaluates Action:** The critic evaluates the chosen action by estimating the value ($Q(s, a)$) using the experience (state, action, reward) collected from the environment.

3. **Policy Update:** The policy in the actor is updated based on the difference between the critic's estimated value ($Q(s, a)$) and the actual reward received (R) from the environment. This difference, known as the temporal difference (TD) error, guides the policy update in a direction that promotes actions leading to higher rewards.

Advantages of Actor-Critic Methods:

- **Sample Efficiency:** By leveraging the value function

estimates from the critic, actor-critic methods can be more sample-efficient compared to pure policy gradient methods, requiring fewer interactions with the environment to learn effectively.

- **Reduced Variance:** The critic's value estimates can help reduce the variance in the policy gradient update, leading to more stable learning.

Popular Actor-Critic Architectures:

- **Deep Deterministic Policy Gradients (DDPG):** A powerful DRL architecture well-suited for continuous control tasks. DDPG utilizes both actor and critic networks that are deep neural networks, enabling them to learn complex relationships in high-dimensional environments.
- **Advantage Actor-Critic (A2C):** A variant that introduces the concept of advantage estimation, which focuses on the advantage of an action compared to the

average action within a state. This can further improve the learning efficiency.

In Conclusion:

Actor-critic methods offer a compelling approach to RL by combining the strengths of policy gradients and value functions. By leveraging the critic's value estimates, actor-critic methods achieve sample efficiency and mitigate variance issues, leading to effective RL agents capable of tackling complex tasks. As we delve deeper into advanced RL topics, we'll encounter more applications of actor-critic methods and their impact on the field.

8.3 Multi-Agent Reinforcement Learning: Learning Coordination and Cooperation

Multi-agent reinforcement learning (MARL) introduces a fascinating extension to the world of RL by introducing multiple agents into the learning process. These agents can collaborate to achieve a common goal (cooperative MARL) or compete against each other (competitive MARL). Compared to single-agent RL, MARL presents unique challenges and opportunities, requiring agents to develop strategies for coordination and communication to succeed.

Scenarios for Multi-Agent RL:

Imagine the following scenarios:

- A team of self-driving cars navigating a highway needs to cooperate to ensure safe and efficient traffic flow (cooperative MARL).
- Two teams of robots compete in a simulated soccer game, requiring strategic decision-making and

coordinated actions (competitive MARL).

- Multiple robots collaborate to assemble a complex object in a factory, where each robot needs to learn its role and how to interact effectively with the others (cooperative MARL).

Challenges in Multi-Agent RL:

- **Non-Stationary Environments:** The environment dynamics become non-stationary due to the actions of other agents. The reward an agent receives depends not only on its own actions but also on the actions of others, making it a complex learning problem.

- **Need for Coordination and Communication:** Agents need to develop mechanisms to coordinate their actions and potentially communicate with each other to achieve a common goal or outperform their opponents.

- **Credit Assignment:** Determining which agent deserves credit for the achieved outcome (positive reward) or blame (negative reward) can be challenging, especially in scenarios with many agents and complex interactions.

Approaches to Multi-Agent RL:

Several approaches have been developed to address the challenges of MARL:

- **Centralized Training, Decentralized Execution (CTDE):** During training, a central entity has access to the global state of all agents and can compute optimal joint actions. However, at execution time, agents only receive local observations and act independently based on their learned policies.

- **Multi-Agent Deep Q-learning (MADDQN):** Extends DQN to the multi-agent setting, where each agent learns a Q-value function for its own actions, but also considers the actions of other agents when making decisions.

- **Policy Gradient Methods in MARL:** Techniques like Actor-Critic can be adapted for MARL scenarios, with modifications to address the challenges of non-stationary environments and credit assignment.

Communication in MARL:

The concept of communication between agents is an active area of research in MARL. Some approaches involve allowing agents to share limited information through pre-defined signals or learned communication protocols. This opens doors for exploring cooperative behaviors that require more sophisticated coordination and information exchange between agents.

Conclusion:

Multi-agent reinforcement learning presents a captivating frontier in RL. By addressing the challenges of coordination, communication, and credit assignment, MARL opens doors to developing intelligent agents that can collaborate or compete effectively in complex, multi-agent environments. As research in MARL progresses, we can expect even more innovative approaches and applications to emerge in various domains.

Chapter 9: Deployment and Evaluation: Bringing Your RL Agent to Life

Congratulations! You've trained a reinforcement learning (RL) agent, and it's performing well in the simulated environment. But the journey doesn't end here. In this chapter, we'll delve into the crucial aspects of deploying your RL agent to the real world and evaluating its effectiveness in practical applications.

9.1 Deployment Considerations: Bridging the Gap from Simulation to Reality

Deploying an RL agent to the real world necessitates careful consideration of several factors:

- **Reality Gap:** The agent's performance in the simulated environment might not directly translate to the real world due to factors like sensor noise, actuator limitations, and unforeseen circumstances.
- **Safety Considerations:** If the agent interacts with the physical world (e.g., robotics),

safety measures must be prioritized to prevent harm or damage.

- **Computational Resources:** The computational demands of running the RL agent in the real world might be higher than in simulation. Ensure you have adequate computing power for real-time decision-making.

Strategies for Mitigating the Reality Gap:

- **Sim-to-Real Transfer Techniques:** Leverage techniques like domain randomization (introducing variations in the simulation environment) to improve the agent's adaptability to real-world situations.

- **Continual Learning:** In real-world scenarios, the environment might continue to change over time. Employ continual learning techniques so the agent can adapt and improve its performance based on new experiences.

9.2 Evaluation Metrics: Measuring Success in the Real World

Evaluating an RL agent's performance in the real world is crucial to assess its effectiveness and identify areas for improvement. Here are some key metrics to consider:

- **Task Completion Rate:** Measures the percentage of times the agent successfully achieves the desired goal.
- **Average Reward:** Tracks the average reward obtained by the agent over time.
- **Efficiency Metrics:** In some cases, metrics like time taken to complete a task or resource consumption might be important.
- **Human Evaluation:** Involve human experts to evaluate

the agent's behavior based on qualitative factors like smoothness, efficiency, or safety (in robotics applications).

Beyond the Numbers:

While metrics provide valuable insights, it's essential to consider the broader context:

- **Safety:** Ensure the agent operates safely in the real world, especially during deployment in safety-critical domains.
- **Interpretability:** If possible, strive to understand the

agent's decision-making process to identify potential biases or unintended consequences.

- **Ethical Considerations:** Be mindful of ethical implications, especially when deploying RL agents in scenarios that might impact people's lives.

9.3 Case Studies: Real-World Applications of RL

Here are some inspiring examples of how RL is making waves in various domains:

- **Robotics:** RL agents are being trained to control robots for tasks like manipulation, navigation, and assembly.

- **Recommendation Systems:** RL can personalize recommendations on e-commerce platforms or streaming services.
- **Resource Management:** RL algorithms can optimize resource allocation in complex systems like traffic networks or power grids.
- **Game Playing:** RL agents have achieved superhuman performance in challenging games like Go and StarCraft II.

9.4 Conclusion: The Future of Reinforcement Learning

The field of RL is rapidly evolving, with continuous advancements in algorithms, hardware capabilities, and theoretical foundations. As we move forward, we can expect to see even more remarkable applications of RL agents that can:

- **Operate in complex and uncertain environments**
- **Continuously learn and adapt**
- **Collaborate effectively with humans**

Reinforcement learning holds immense potential to revolutionize various industries and domains. By carefully considering deployment strategies, evaluation techniques, and ethical implications, we can ensure that RL agents bring positive advancements to our world.

Chapter 10: The Future of Reinforcement Learning: What Lies Ahead?

The captivating realm of reinforcement learning (RL) is brimming with potential, and the future promises even more groundbreaking advancements. In this chapter, we'll explore some exciting frontiers that are poised to shape the trajectory of RL in the years to come.

10.1 Emerging Trends and Advancements: Shaping the Future of RL

The realm of reinforcement learning (RL) is undergoing a

period of rapid evolution, with new ideas and advancements constantly emerging. In this section, we'll delve into some of the most promising trends that are poised to shape the future of RL and unlock its full potential:

1. Sample-Efficient Reinforcement Learning:

- Overcoming the data bottleneck is crucial for making RL more practical. Here are some key trends:
  - **Meta-Reinforcement Learning:** Meta-RL algorithms aim to train agents that can learn how

to learn quickly. By learning across multiple related tasks, the agent can adapt to new situations with less data required for each specific task.

- **Model-Based Reinforcement Learning:** By incorporating models of the environment into the learning process, agents can perform "simulations" internally, reducing the need for real-world interactions to learn effectively.

- ○ **Offline Reinforcement Learning:** This approach leverages pre-collected datasets to train RL agents, eliminating the need for online interaction with the environment during the learning process. This can be particularly valuable when real-world interaction is expensive or time-consuming.

2. Lifelong Learning for RL Agents:

- The ability to continuously learn and adapt throughout their operational lifetime is essential for RL agents. This is particularly important in real-world scenarios where environments are constantly evolving. Key advancements include:
  - **Continual Learning Techniques:** These techniques enable agents to learn from new experiences without forgetting previously learned knowledge. This is crucial for adapting to

changes in the environment without compromising past learnings.

- **Online Reinforcement Learning with Model Adaptation:** By continuously updating the internal model of the environment, agents can adjust their decision-making to reflect the evolving dynamics of the real world.

3. Reinforcement Learning for Robotics:

- The synergy between RL and robotics is a powerful force for innovation. Here's how RL is transforming robotics:
  - **Multi-Objective Reinforcement Learning:** Robots can be trained to handle complex tasks with multiple objectives, such as manipulation, navigation, and object recognition, all within a single RL framework.
  - **Hierarchical Reinforcement Learning for Robots:** By

decomposing complex tasks into smaller, manageable subtasks, robots can learn more efficient and robust policies for real-world robotic applications.

4. Reinforcement Learning in the Cloud:

- Cloud computing platforms offer vast computational resources and large-scale data storage capabilities, ideal for training complex RL models. Cloud-based RL presents several advantages:

- **Scalability:** Cloud platforms enable training on massive datasets and complex models, which can lead to significant performance improvements in RL agents.
- **Remote Access and Collaboration:** Cloud-based RL facilitates collaboration among researchers and engineers by providing shared access to training infrastructure and data.

5. The Intersection of RL and Other AI Fields:

- Cross-pollination between RL and other areas of AI is leading to exciting advancements:
  - **Reinforcement Learning and Natural Language Processing (NLP):** RL agents that can comprehend and generate natural language open doors for more natural human-agent interaction and potentially AI-powered chatbots with enhanced capabilities.

- **Reinforcement Learning and Computer Vision (CV):** Integrating RL with CV allows agents to learn directly from visual inputs, enabling them to navigate environments, grasp objects, and perform tasks that require visual perception.

Conclusion

These emerging trends represent just a glimpse into the exciting future of reinforcement learning. As research continues to push the boundaries, we can expect RL to play an increasingly important role in various sectors, from robotics and automation to healthcare and scientific discovery. The potential of RL to revolutionize the way we interact with machines and the world around us is truly remarkable.

10.2 The Ethical Considerations of Reinforcement Learning: Ensuring Responsible Development

The power of reinforcement learning (RL) comes hand-in-hand with the responsibility to ensure its ethical development and deployment. As RL agents become more sophisticated and integrated into real-world applications, it's crucial to consider the ethical implications and establish safeguards to mitigate potential risks.

Key Ethical Concerns in RL:

- **Bias and Fairness:** RL algorithms can inherit and amplify biases present in the data they are trained on. This can lead to discriminatory outcomes, especially in domains like loan approvals or hiring decisions.
- **Safety and Control:** When interacting with the physical world (e.g., robotics), RL

agents must be designed with safety as a top priority. Robust control mechanisms are needed to prevent unintended harm or damage.

- **Transparency and Explainability:** As RL models become more complex, understanding their decision-making processes becomes increasingly challenging. A lack of transparency can hinder trust and accountability, especially in safety-critical applications.
- **Misaligned Goals and Reward Functions:** Carefully

crafted reward functions are essential for guiding the agent's behavior. However, poorly designed reward functions can lead to unintended consequences if the agent exploits loopholes or prioritizes the reward over ethical considerations.

Promoting Ethical RL Development:

Here are some crucial steps towards ensuring the responsible development and deployment of RL:

- **Fairness in Data and Algorithms:** Employ techniques to mitigate bias in training data and develop algorithms less susceptible to inheriting and amplifying these biases.
- **Formal Verification and Safety Measures:** Utilize formal verification techniques to prove the safety properties of RL agents and implement robust safety mechanisms to prevent harm in real-world scenarios.
- **Human Oversight and Explainability Tools:**

Maintain human oversight in critical decision-making processes and invest in developing explainability tools to shed light on the rationale behind an agent's actions.

- **Alignment of Goals and Values:** Carefully design reward functions that promote ethical behavior and align with broader societal values. Open discussions and collaborations between RL developers, ethicists, and policymakers are essential for establishing ethical guidelines

for RL development and
deployment.

Conclusion

The ethical considerations
surrounding RL are complex and
require ongoing attention. By
fostering open dialogue,
prioritizing fairness and safety,
and adhering to ethical
principles, we can ensure that RL
is developed and utilized
responsibly for the benefit of
society. As RL continues to
evolve, the onus lies on
researchers, developers, and
policymakers to work together to
navigate the ethical landscape

and ensure that this powerful technology is used for good.

10.3 Your Next Steps: A Roadmap for Continuous Learning and Innovation

Congratulations! You've embarked on a thrilling journey into the captivating world of reinforcement learning (RL). This chapter serves as a launchpad for your continued exploration and contribution to this dynamic field. Here are some inspiring pathways to fuel your passion for RL and empower you to become a lifelong learner and innovator:

1. Deepen Your Theoretical Understanding:

- Delve deeper into the theoretical foundations of RL. Explore advanced topics like multi-objective RL, hierarchical RL, and continuous control.
- Strengthen your mathematical background relevant to RL, including linear algebra, probability theory, and optimization techniques.
- Participate in online courses or university programs specializing in RL to gain a

comprehensive understanding of the field.

2. Hone Your Coding Skills:

- Practice implementing RL algorithms from scratch using popular deep learning frameworks like TensorFlow or PyTorch. This hands-on experience will solidify your grasp of the underlying concepts.
- Explore open-source RL libraries and frameworks like OpenAI Gym, Stable Baselines3, and DeepMind Lab. These tools provide pre-built environments and

algorithms, allowing you to experiment with various RL approaches efficiently.

- Contribute to open-source RL projects on platforms like GitHub. This not only enhances your coding skills but also allows you to collaborate with the RL community.

3. Engage in Real-World Projects:

- Identify a real-world problem that can potentially benefit from RL. This could be anything from optimizing resource allocation in a network to training an AI agent to play a complex game.

- Formulate a research question or hypothesis related to your chosen problem. How can RL be applied to address this challenge?

- Gather relevant data or create a simulation environment for your project. Utilize tools like robotic simulators or game engines to set up realistic scenarios for your RL agent.

- Train and evaluate your RL agent. Analyze the results and iterate on your approach to improve performance. Document your findings and share them with the RL community through blog posts, research papers, or conference presentations.

4. Stay Updated with the Latest Advancements:

- Follow prominent researchers and institutions working in the field of RL. Attend conferences and workshops related to RL to stay abreast of cutting-edge developments.

- Subscribe to online publications and forums dedicated to RL. Engage in discussions with other learners and experts to broaden your knowledge and perspectives.
- Consider pursuing research opportunities in RL labs or universities. Contributing to ongoing research projects is an excellent way to push the boundaries of the field and make a significant impact.

5. Foster a Growth Mindset:

- Embrace challenges as opportunities to learn and grow. The field of RL is constantly evolving, so a willingness to adapt and learn new things is essential.
- Don't be afraid to experiment and make mistakes. Often, the most significant breakthroughs stem from failures and unexpected discoveries.
- Network with other RL enthusiasts and collaborate on projects. Sharing ideas and learning from others can

significantly accelerate your progress.

The Future of RL is in Your Hands

The potential of reinforcement learning is vast and continues to unfold. By following these steps and fostering a passion for lifelong learning, you can become an active contributor to the future of RL. As you explore, experiment, and innovate, remember that the journey itself is as rewarding as the destination. Embrace the challenges, celebrate the breakthroughs, and be part of the exciting evolution of RL!